Powerful And Effective

Teaching on Prayer

Bonnie Inkster

Copyright © 2018 Bonnie Inkster

Published by 5 Smooth Stones
The right of Bonnie Inkster to be identified as the author of the Work has been asserted by her in accordance with the Copyright, Designs and Patents Act 1988 All rights reserved. No part of this publication may be reproduced, stored in a retrieval system, or transmitted, in any form or by any means without the prior permission of the publisher, nor be otherwise circulated in any form of binding or cover other than that in which it is published and without a similar condition being imposed on the subsequent purchaser.

Kelowna, BC
Canada

All rights reserved.

ISBN-13: 978-1-9994251-1-1

DEDICATION

I dedicate this to Jim, my husband who is
my friend, my encourager, the one who
has stood by me and said, 'You go girl!
You can do it!" You have led me into
truth and I love you dearly.

CONTENTS

OTHER RESOURCES BY BONNIE AND JIM INKSTER

24 SECRETS TO GREAT PARENTING: TRIED, TESTED AND TRUE

THE CHRISTMAS STORY

FAITH - THE CURRENCY OF HEAVEN

GIVING: GOD'S HEART IN YOU

THE GAME (FOR 9-12 YEAR OLDS)

THE WONDER WORKER: JESUS IN THE BOOK OF MARK

UNDER HIS WINGS: PSALM 91: A DEVOTIONAL

EYES OF WONDER

Bonnie Inkster

1. Our Righteousness

The book of James 5:16b says that the prayer of a righteous person is powerful and effective. The first thing that needs to be established is that word righteous. At one time this was a stumbling block for me. Was I righteous enough to rank among the powerful and effective?

What if I got mad at my kids? Said something that was judgmental or critical? What if I hadn't read my Bible or gone to church? Am I still righteous or at least righteous

> When our life is in Him, we are righteous

enough to pray effectively? We need to settle the issue of who is righteous!

The bible tells us in Romans 3:10 that there is no one righteous, no not one! So isn't it good that the requirement for righteousness is found in Jesus! Jesus took all our sin, transgressions and iniquities on the cross. He paid the price for our sins so we could be free. When we receive Jesus into our heart we become a new creature in Christ according to Romans

5:17. This new creature is righteous because He is righteous. 2 Corinthians 5:21 puts it this way, "He made him who knew no sin to be sin on our behalf, so that we might become the righteousness of God in Him". He is our righteousness and because our life is now in Him we are righteous. If you are born again, Jesus lives in you, your sins are washed away and you are without spot or wrinkle! In other words, you are righteous! Titus puts it this way: "it's not by works of righteousness that we have done but because of his mercy. He saved us through the washing of rebirth and the renewal of the Holy Spirit".

Being righteous does not mean that the Holy Spirit will not speak to you about something that needs to change. He is in the business of setting us free and transforming us into the image of Christ. However, in the spirit you are still righteous! The enemy will come and test this truth. When you go to pray he might try to tell you that you aren't worthy or holy enough. Don't be tricked by the devil. He is the father of lies. He tempts and he condemns. Remember, your Heavenly Father is full of compassion and abounding in love. Hebrews 4:16 states, 'Let us approach God's throne of grace with confidence, so that we may receive mercy and grace in our time of need". Notice the word 'confidence' in this scripture. Confidence is the state of feeling certain about the truth of something. You can be assured that God's word is truth. You will always find mercy and grace when you need it because you are the righteousness of God in Christ Jesus our Lord.

This issue must be settled in our minds before we can be confident that our prayers are powerful and effective. But why are our prayers so powerful? That answer is simple. We serve a mighty God who is all-powerful. Psalm 147:5 say, "great is the Lord and mighty in power". Romans 1:20 explains God has two invisible qualities - his eternal power and his divine nature. Jehoshaphat says of the Lord in 2 Chronicles 20:6 that in God's hands are power and might so that none can withstand you. The power of God changes people, heals sickness, alters circumstances, it causes demons to flee, nations to be transformed and spiritual atmospheres to shift. We need to know that it is God's power that is released when we pray.

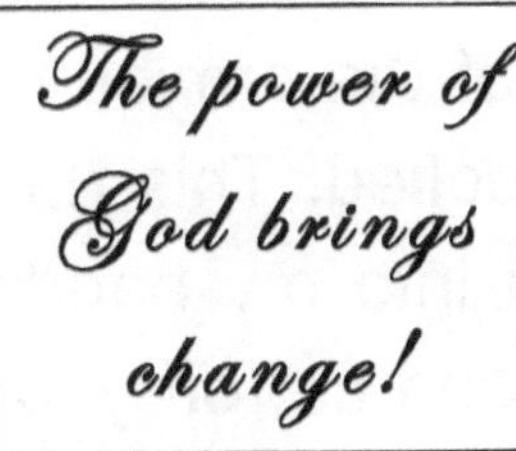

King David knew that he could rely on the power of God to flow through him. He said to Goliath, "you come against me with sword and spear and javelin but I come against you in the name of the Lord Almighty, the God of the armies of Israel, whom you have defied. This day the Lord will deliver you into my hands and I'll strike you down and cut off your head". David went on to say, "all who are gathered there would know that it was not by sword or spear that the Lord saves; for the battle is the Lord's and he will give all of you into our hands". David's actions in the natural are like our prayers. He had the confidence to know that God was with him and faith to know that nothing is too difficult for him. This giant that young David was facing was huge. But David had his perspective in the right place. His eyes were clearly on God knowing that nothing is too difficult for Him. Paul says it this way, "I can do all thing through Christ". So when we pray we can be assured that the powerful hand of God will be moved. Therefore, our prayers are powerful!

The verse in James 5 not only states that our prayers are powerful but they are effective. Effective is defined as being successful in producing a desired or intended result. I like the King James Version that says our prayers "availeth much". We need to know that prayer gets results. What a complete waste of time it would be if we did not believe that prayer works! Over and over in the Psalms we read that the people called out to the Lord and he heard them and delivered them from all their troubles.

Because you are the righteousness of God in Christ Jesus, when you pray, you are powerful and your prayers are effective.

𝒲. Hearing

Romans 8:14 says that for those who are led by the Spirit of God are the children of God. In other words, if you are a child of God you are lead by His Spirit. In John 10:27 Jesus puts it this way, 'my sheep hear my voice or listen to my voice; I know them and they follow me'. It is important for you to know that first off you are a child of the King and that because you are you have access to Him. You have been wired to hear the voice of God! How exciting is that! Not only are you wired to hear his voice but you also get to participate in His divine plan to bring His kingdom here on earth as it is in heaven.

Jesus was led by the Spirit in all He did. At His baptism the Holy Spirit descended on Him in the form of a dove and a voice came from heaven: 'You are my Son, whom I love; with you I am well pleased'. (Mark 1:11) The Father spoke to Jesus in an audible voice! Note that the Father was well pleased with Jesus before He ever did a thing. He was loved just because He was His son! I remember holding my children and my grandchildren. I loved them; they were such a gift, so beautiful, such a blessing! They hadn't done anything to earn my love; I just loved them and was so grateful for each of their lives. In the same way your heavenly Father loves you. You don't have to do anything. He loves you just because you are His child!

However, you see in Mark 1:12 that the next thing that Jesus did was follow the Spirit's leading. Throughout Jesus' life He followed the lead of the Holy Spirit. In Mark 5:19 Jesus states it this way, 'the Son can do

His voice may feel like an impression, idea or a thought.

nothing by Himself; he can do only what he sees his Father doing because whatever the Father does the Son also does'. The way Jesus sees what the Father is doing is by the Spirit. The Holy Spirit leads and guides us; He unveils the will and desires of the Father to us. It is then our responsibility to follow or obey the lead.

The ways in which the Spirit speaks and leads are countless. This can be a very individual experience but I will look at a few. First off, the Spirit speaks to us all through a still small voice. You can hear Him speak to you internally. It doesn't sound like a harsh uncommon voice but like your own. At times it may feel like an impression, idea or a thought that rolls through your mind. You might be washing the dishes and suddenly think of a person. You could wonder how they are doing and leave it at that or you could pick up the prompt of the Spirit and pray for them right then. Ask the Spirit if you need to pray in a specific way or you might call them or send them a note of some kind. The point is the Spirit is speaking to us in many ways. The more you respond the more you will become aware of what ways He is speaking to you.

I remember on one occasion when Jim had taken a team of young men to the Philippines and among them was our youngest son who was 13 at the time. I was at home and felt prompted to pray for their protection. At that time the group was in a Jollibee (a fast food restaurant similar to McDonalds). Jim was going up the stairs and heard my voice calling him. He actually turned around to see if I was there. Realizing it was not me in person he asked the Lord what He was saying. The Lord spoke to him clearly and said to be careful of the women. He thought it had to do with the young men he had with him but as it turned out there was an aggressive assignment on our young son. The woman both young and old thought he was very "guapo". He is indeed handsome but at 13 it was not what we expected. At one point in a shopping mall a group of young women came between Jim and him, grabbing his hand and dragging him off down the mall. He managed to shake off the girls' grip and run back to

You need to rest in the fact that He is the one that is leading you.

his father. From there on he took the word very seriously too. We are very grateful for the leading of the Spirit and His hand of protection upon our lives.

When the Lord leads you to pray for someone or a situation you need to rest in the fact that He is the one that is leading you. Therefore, you do what He is doing, what is on the Father's heart at that time. He only requires us to act in partnership with Him; the results are up to Him! I remember Justin Cornwall saying that the Lord invited him to go to Brazil. His response was, 'well Lord, I have never wanted to go there'. The Lord said to him, 'well, I'm going with or without you. Do you want to come?' That really hit me! God is constantly on the move and He invites us to join Him! How exciting that the Lord of the universe asks us along and moves through humanity to change the world.

As I said, there are many ways that the Spirit can direct or speak to you. When we gather as a group to seek the Lord for direction we will often still our minds and ask the Holy Spirit to come and speak. We will then worship. If there is someone with an instrument anointed to lead worship, great. If not, then we use what is available like mp3 recordings. The point is that God inhabits the praises of his people. Before Elisha prophesied as recorded in 2 Kings 3:15 he called for a harpist. The worship brought the Spirit and the word of the Lord came forth. Does this mean that every time you hear from the Lord you need worship first? NO!! The Spirit directs in many ways but this is one way to corporately lead a group to receive from the Lord. It takes your mind off earthly things and directs your attention to the Lord for the direction you are seeking.

Through this worship time people may have different experiences. Not everyone hears in the same way. One might get a scripture, another may see a picture or have an impression of something or have an open vision. Everything is valuable and nothing should be ignored. The point is we are looking to be directed or spoken to. A word may require investigation and interpretation. Proverbs 25:2 says, 'it is the glory of God to conceal a matter; to search out a matter is the glory of kings'. Google is a handy tool but not the only way to investigate. It is inspiring when you follow the leading of the Spirit and uncover a nugget!

The next step after hearing what is on the Father's heart is to begin to pray into what you have heard. One never knows exactly what will happen as a result. However, we do know that God is good and His will is always good. Therefore, we can say come Holy Spirit, direct our paths and our prayers; shift the atmosphere, change culture, draw people to yourself, heal the broken hearted, set the captives free, heal and loose salvation throughout the nations! YOUR KINGDOM COME ON EARTH AS IT IS IN HEAVEN!!!

In the next chapters we will discuss ways to pray that will produce results.

𝒮. Humility

I remember a song that said you are God and I am not! How profound! When it comes to prayer one of the keys is found in this truth. Because I am not God my place is a place of humility. The word 'humility' means having the quality of having a modest or low view of one's importance. We are told in Philippians 2 that we should have the same mindset as Christ who did not consider equality with God something to be grasped but humbled himself and took on the very nature of a servant. As a result, God exalted him to the highest place and gave him the name that is above every name, that name being Jesus Christ our Lord.

In 1 Peter 5:6 and again in James 4:10 we are told to humble ourselves under the mighty hand of God and he will lift you up. Why do we humble ourselves? Because God resists the proud but gives grace or favour to the humble. This is all about

Because I am not God my place is a place of humility.

the condition of the heart. Calling on the Lord shows that you submit to His authority and ability to answer your prayer. He is greater so I submit to him. If we didn't believe that God would answer our prayer than why waste the time praying. But we believe that with God all things are possible, that he is able to move the mountains in front of me and make a way where there is no way. Knowing this, we bow low under His mighty hand knowing that He will do exceedingly above and beyond all we dare think or even ask.

1 Chronicles 7:14 says that if my people who are called by my name, will humble themselves and pray and seek my face and turn from their wicked ways, then I will hear from heaven, and I will forgive their sins and heal their land. When

praying for your city, country or in the nations humility is always the starting place. It is easy to see with our natural eyes the decay in the fabric of our nations. We must see it from the place of a bended knee. If we stand with judgment in our hearts, God will oppose us. But when we humble ourselves before Him, He will hear from heaven and heal the land.

I am not suggesting that you go around beating yourself but rather that you come before the Father and ask him what He wants you to pray about. Always keep in your mind that mercy triumphs over judgment (James 2:13). That's why Jesus came, God so loved the world that He gave His only begotten son. Jesus took all the world's sin, iniquity and transgressions upon himself that we would be free.

Ezekiel 22:30 says, "I looked for someone among them who would build up the wall and stand before me in the gap on behalf of the land so I would not have to destroy it, but I found no one." Notice the words 'build up'. We are called to build up and in order to do that we must take our place by humbly standing in the breach in the wall.

Bonnie Inkster

4. Authority

Jesus said in Luke 10:19 that he has given us authority to trample on snakes and scorpions and to overcome all the power of the enemy and then continues to say nothing will harm you. Authority is defined as the power or right to give orders, make decisions and enforce obedience. When you have authority, you have official permission and the right to act in a specific way. Authority is given or delegated to a person from another.

If we look at this definition and the bible, we will see what we have been given, who gave it to us and how we use it. First off we see that Jesus has delegated authority to us. The scripture in Luke 10 tells us that he gave 72 disciples authority and sent them out to heal the sick and preach the kingdom of God is near. In the same way in Matthew 28:18 in what is known as the great commission Jesus states that all authority has been given to him. He then goes on to say to us, 'now you go and make disciples of all nations'. Jesus was given authority when He defeated the devil on the cross. He disarmed the powers and authorities and made a public spectacle of them. By doing this, He triumphed over them. As a result Jesus was given all power and authority and he in turn has delegated it to us as we walk in humility. If you are born again you have authority.

So what do we have authority over? In Luke 10 it tells us that we have authority over snakes and scorpions and to overcome all the power of the enemy. He is not speaking of physical snakes and scorpions. Jesus does not mean we need to handle snakes and scorpions to validate our

> *If you are born again you have authority*

authority. That would be foolish. He is speaking of terms used to describe Satan and his cronies. Strong's concordance points out that the word 'pateo', translated snake, in Luke 10 means: the serpent, which deceived Eve, was regarded by the Jews as the devil. Jesus said we could tread upon the snakes, scorpions and all the power of the enemy. The word 'tread' from Strong's means 'to trample, crush with the feet or to advance by setting foot upon, tread upon: to encounter successfully the greatest perils from the machinations and persecutions with which Satan would fain thwart the preaching of the gospel'.

The word, machinations, is defined as a scheme or a plot. We are warned by Paul not to be unaware of the enemy's schemes. The enemy is plotting and planning against you and me. Why? To stop the advancement of the kingdom of God!

Jesus said that he came to destroy the works of the evil one. (1 John 3:8) That was Jesus purpose when he came to earth. John 10:10 describes the enemy as a thief and says that the thief comes only to steal, kill and destroy. The good news comes in the later part of this scripture when Jesus says 'but I have come to bring life and that more abundantly'. Any time you see destruction happening you know who is at the root of it. You see God is good and He brings life. The enemy has different names but his sting is full of poison. However, we have been given authority over him. Only we need to exercise the authority we have been given.

We have a friend who was a police office in London England. He told us of the first time he had to stop traffic in the city. He really didn't know how he was going to do it. The traffic was thick and heavy but he stepped out into the middle of it and put up His hand. Guess what happened...exactly, right away all the traffic stopped. You see he had to use the authority he had been given. And so it is with us. We can be in the midst of a dreadful situation but Mark 11 says if we speak to the mountain it will be removed.

Jesus said to Peter in Matthew 16:19 that He would give Peter the keys to the

Kingdom of Heaven. Then he went on to say whatever you bind on earth will be bound in heaven and whatever you loosed on earth will be loosed in heaven. In other words we need to use our authority to bring His kingdom and establish it on earth as well as displacing the enemy's kingdom. Jesus said in the Lord's Prayer, "your kingdom come, your will be done!"

We have been given all authority, but authority creates responsibility. In other words we have the ability to respond. When Jesus encountered a demon he either rebuked it, commanded it to be quiet or said come out. When someone was ill, He may have said be healed, stretch out your hand, pick up your mat or maybe He spat in their eyes. When the storm was threatening He rebuked the wind and waves. When the people tried to throw Him off a cliff He walked right through the crowd unharmed. There are many ways the enemy will try to come at us. He will want to poison or sting your life. Like Jesus we need to use our authority over the evil one and invite the kingdom of God to prevail. Remember, if you walk in humility under delegated authority, then nothing will be impossible for you!

5. Agreement, Unity, Faith

I have said many times that I would rather pray with one person in agreement than a hundred who are not. Why? There is power in agreement. The word agreement sounds self-explanatory but agreement denotes harmony or accordance in opinion or feeling. It is a position or result of like-mindedness. Take note of the word 'accordance'. When the Holy Spirit came to those in the upper room they were all in one accord. In other words they were in agreement. There was harmony in the room. There wasn't a few of them saying 'what are we waiting for' or others saying 'this is a waste of time'. That would have produced disharmony. It's always disturbing listening to an orchestra tuning up because it creates a sense of chaos and discord that is jarring to the nerves and the hall. But once they begin to follow the conductor and they work together there is harmony and the result is beautiful music! Romans 12:16 says 'live in harmony with each other'. When you do, you have agreement and then you can expect the Spirit to move.

We must remember that prayer is a spiritual business. In Matthew 18:19-20 Jesus says, "again I tell you that if two of you agree about anything they ask for, it will be done for them by my Father in heaven. For where two or three gather in my name, there am I with them". If our prayers are to be effective we need agreement. Where there is agreement there is faith. When we agree together, the Father will answer. Because prayer is spiritual, it is necessary to act in faith because without faith it's impossible to please God. But according to Hebrews 11:6 "anyone that comes to him must believe that he exists and that he is a rewarded of those who diligently seek him".

This is the first step to agreement. God is a rewarder of those that earnestly seek him so when two agree in faith there is power. I am not negating or ignoring the prayer of one righteous person. Abraham, the father of our faith, was alone when he persuaded God through intercession to spare Sodom and Gomorrah if there were 10 righteous people living there. That too is powerful and effective but I am sharing a biblical principle of agreement. It says in Deuteronomy 32:30 that one can chase a thousand and two, ten thousand. It is a multiplication concept.

We see this principle in motion at the Tower of Babel in Genesis 11. The people spoke one language and had a common speech. They decided to build for themselves a tower that reached to the heavens. Listen to the Lord's response in verse six, "If as one people speaking the same language they have begun to do this, then nothing they plan to do will be impossible for them". That is the power of agreement!

Psalm 133 says, "it is good and pleasant for brothers to dwell together in unity for where there is unity there is a commanded blessing". How wonderful it is to pray in a place where there is no strife, no contention, or no doubt that God answers our prayers and no questioning as to whether we can really ask God for something. Paul puts it this way in Philippians 2:2 "be like minded, having the same love, being one in the spirit and of one mind".

When we pray in agreement with faith in our hearts, we can be assured that the Father hears our prayers. That is why it is so important to guard the unity of our faith because the enemy will always come and try to bring discord and strife. God has given us everything we need against the plans and power of the enemy.

6. The Word

The word of God is an effective weapon to use in pray. When Jesus was being tempted by the devil he said that man shall not live on bread alone but by every word that proceeds from the mouth of God. Psalm 119 says that your word is a lamp unto my feet and a light unto my path. While Jeremiah says that the word is like a fire and a hammer. We are told in Hebrews 1:3 that God sustains everything by His word and Jesus said his words will never pass away. Hebrews 4:12 says the word of God is living and active. Some translations say it's alive and powerful, sharper than a double-edged sword.

When I think about something that is living or alive, I see movement and life. The dictionary defines alive as the state of action, full of activity and having life. The word of God is full of action. It is powerful and will accomplish what it's been sent to do according to Isaiah 55:11. God's word is

His word is alive!

not without power, it will hit the mark and achieve the desired result. In Genesis 1 we read that God said or God spoke and the heavens were formed. God created by speaking. Your words hold the power of life and death (Proverbs 18:21). You are created in the image of God. Your tongue has power but how much more power when you speak the word of God into a situation.

Ephesians 6 tells us that the word of God is the sword of the Spirit. When it comes to prayer the word of God is crucial. Jesus quoted the word to the devil when he was being tempted, when he was on trial and when he was teaching the disciples. Because the word of God is active, alive and powerful, we need to pick it up and speak it out. If I am in a tense situation, I speak the word into it. Like a sword it breaks through the barriers or the harassment I may be experiencing.

On the other hand all the promises of God are yes and amen in Christ Jesus. Therefore I can declare the word of God prophetically and see His blessing released in my life or whatever I am praying for. In Ezekiel 37 we find Ezekiel having an encounter with the Spirit of God. All Ezekiel can see is a valley of dry bones but God has a plan and a destiny for these dry bones. God says to prophesy to these bones and He will make breath enter them and they will come to life.

This is exactly what the Lord is saying to us today. Pick up that sword of the Spirit and fight. Fight the good fight of faith and wield your sword. Speak His word over situations and see life come where there is destruction and death. Speak the word of God out. Don't look at what you presently see but be assured that the word of God will accomplish the good work it's been sent to do.

Bonnie Inkster

7. Renounce

I want to share with you a very, very powerful word to use in prayers. RENOUNCE! For many, the word renounce feels like a harsh word. However, put in the right context, and with the right understanding, the word renounce has power. We first need to define the word to grasp the meaning. Renounce means to give up ownership, to resign a right or position, to declare one's abandonment of a claim, right or possession on something or someone.

2 Corinthians 4:2 says, "we have renounced secret and shameful ways". In other words when it comes to sin we repent, renouncing whatever it is that is in opposition to God. For example, the Lord many be speaking to you about something in your life that needs to change. I remember the time the Lord spoke to me about exaggeration. I would go to an event and it would be the biggest or best or there would be tons of people there. The Lord said I was lying! Harsh! But once I had the revelation that I was not speaking truth I repented for exaggerating and renounced it. I gave

up ownership of it and cut off any hold it would have over my life. Because I am conscious of this in my life, I am careful with quoting numbers and facts and I try to qualify something by saying I think or maybe.

There is a cost in following

But remember that renounce means to give up ownership. In Luke 14:26 Jesus says, "If anyone comes to me and does not hate their father and mother, wife and children, brothers and sisters - yes, even their own life - such a person cannot be my disciple". Surely Jesus doesn't mean hate when we are told to love one another, honour our fathers and mothers. In the book of Matthew Jesus puts it this way, "anyone who loves their father or mother more than me is not worthy of me; anyone who loves their son or daughter more than me is not worthy of me." These scriptures are followed by pick up you cross and follow me.

There is a cost to following the Lord. One of the costs is keeping an open hand. When relationships hold you back from doing what you are called to do, they have a hold on you. We are called to be free from anything that would entangle us. I have found that the most effective way to stay free is to renounce. I remember when our oldest daughter was leaving us to get married. She wasn't just leaving us she was also moving countries. The ache in my heart was intense. I remember crying and then the Lord spoke to me and personalized Isaiah 40 "comfort,

comfort,… your day of hard service is over". My major input into her life was complete and I needed to renounce her and let her go. God blessed our lives with our children and one by one I had to let them go. Does that mean I don't love them? On the contrary, I love them deeply but I release them into God's hands because I know He has a plan for them, plans to bless them and give them a hope and a future. Too often parents try to control their children's lives. All that will do is end in hardship and resentment. We have taught our family the value of renouncing. We love visiting our children and grandchildren but when we leave we renounce them and give them back to the Lord for it is He that is at work to will and to do according to His good pleasure not ours!

So it is with all relationships. God does not want us dependent on anyone or any thing but Him. If there is someone

> *Renouncing sets you free!*

or something holding you in anyway way the answer is to renounce them or it. I have led people on many prayer trips to loads of places. The prayer times can be invigorating and intense. Upon completing a prayer assignment we renounce the city or country we are in and each other. Why? There are attachments that can happen in the Spirit. So we ask the Holy Spirit to break anything that is attached to us by renouncing the city, the country and people. Other times if we have prayed in a particular spot, we renounce the prayer time there so we can pick up the next place without carrying the concern for the first.

We did a fair bit of hiking when we were kids. I remember coming back home and being checked for ticks and removing any burrs that had attached to us. Then we would wash all our clothes and take a bath. Well, spiritually this is the same concept. We want to remove anything that would stick to us and then say come Holy Spirit and fill us afresh with new revelation for what's next.

When Jim and I leave our hometown to go visit our children or a friend, we renounce the place as we go and take hold of the place we are going to. We ask the Lord to give us wisdom and revelation for the time ahead. I remember a time when our son came home from university. He was having difficulty connecting with his friends, the church and the city and felt like he didn't belong there. He knew something was wrong and it was bothering him. As we began to process this with him the question we asked was: "did you renounce the university and the city when you came home?" "No" was the response. Once we prayed with him, having him renounce the city and the university, we broke the hold it had on him and blessed him to flourish where he was. Guess what? He connected locally. When he went back to university in September he renounced the church, the town that we lived in and us. This allowed him to freely take part in all God had for him at the city where his university was located.

Some of you might be thinking so how do I pray this? It's easy! You say, "Lord, I renounce (naming whatever you need to), I give them to you. I break any hold I have on them or any hold they have on me. I break any ungodly attachment and I ask that you would work in them and me to will and to do according to your good pleasure". The Holy Spirit will show you if there is anything else you need to renounce at this time. All you have to do is ask.

Bonnie Inkster

8. All Sorts of Prayer

I am a firm believer in praying all sorts of prayers and allowing the Spirit to breath on them. Those prayers go to heaven and fill a golden bowl. The angels then place incense in the golden bowl and let that fragrance go up before the Father.

Revelation 8 says that an angel held a golden censer and stood at the altar. He was given much incense to offer along with the prayers of all God's people. The smoke of the incense, together with the prayers of God's people went up before God from the angel's hand. Then the angel took the censer, filled it with fire from the altar and hurled it to the earth...and there came peals of thunder, rumblings, flashes of lightening and an earthquake. In other words those prayers that the people of God prayed made a difference! Something happened, atmospheres shifted. Why? Because prayer moves God to act.

You see your prayers, however feeble they may sound to you, go straight up to the heavens where angels add incense to them and they continue into the Lord's nostrils motivating Him to action. The angels then add fire to them and they produce results. The thought that God smells the incense and is moved is intriguing to me. Jim, my husband and I often walk and pray. The other day we were walking in the morning. I smelled the warmth of the summer morning and it reminded me of a time we were in the Florida Keys over forty years before. That sense of smell brought to my remembrance the days and the wonderful time we had. Well your prayers and intercession will cause the Lord to remember and you will see the results.

Prayer moves God to act.

Take Daniel for example. He was reading the prophecy of Jeremiah and he got the revelation that the seventy years of captivity for the Israelites was over. So in chapter 9 of Daniel we see what he did with the revelation. In the fifth verse of chapter nine we can hear Daniel confessing the sins of the nation. He says we have sinned and done wrong. We have been wicked and rebelled; we have turned away...and he goes on. Notice the word WE. This was 70 years since the exile of the people of Israel to Babylon. Daniel was a teenage boy at the time. He would not have been responsible for the condition of Israel. However, Daniel confessed the sin of the nation before the Lord and said we have sinned and rebelled. In other words, Daniel was not standing in judgment of what transpired but humbled himself before the Lord and confessed the sins as if they were his own.

There are several keys points in this passage. First, we note that Daniel was humble. Humility opens the door to the Father. In

Daniel was not standing in judgment.

the book of James and in 1 Peter we read humble yourselves before the Lord and He will lift you up. God opposes the proud but gives grace to the humble. Humility is profoundly important. Pride is the opposite of humility and God resists or opposes the proud.

Second, there is the key of intercession. Intercession is the action of intervening on the behalf of another. In Ezekiel

22:30 we see that God himself was looking for someone to stand in the gap and build up the wall on behalf of the land but he found no one. The concept of standing in a hole in the wall or the breach in the social fabric of our nations is a foreign concept to many but not to God. He himself took our sins and nailed them to the cross that we might be free. Isaiah 53:12b says that He was numbered with the transgressors for he bore the sins of many and made intercession for the transgressors.

We are called to stand in the gap if we want to see change.

We are called to do likewise. In 1Timothy 2:1 we see that Paul urges us to first of all make petitions, prayers, intercession and thanksgiving for all the people. He also said to the Ephesians to be alert and pray all kinds of prayers for God's people. If we want to see people touched supernaturally by the spirit of God we need to intercede.

A petition is a request or an appeal made to a superior or a judge. For example you might be writing an exam and your petition might be God give me wisdom and understanding. In other words, I need you to help me. Or God protect me as I go, keep me from all evil. It's a request for God to help, heal and intervene. When it is answered it should bring about thanksgiving.

Prayer is talking to God. He hears them

all and like David in the Psalms you can discuss any situation or feeling with Him. In other words it is fellowship or communion with the Father. Jesus was on the mountain all night praying, chances are he made some petitions but more than likely he spent time being with and talking to His

> *If we want to see people touched supernaturally by the spirit of God we need to intercede.*

Father. Paul prayers prayers through his letters to the churches asking God to open eyes, give the spirit of wisdom and revelation, that God would strengthen the inner man. Paul goes on and on throughout his letters with all kinds of prayers and petitions. We need to be encouraged to do likewise.

At this point I feel that it is necessary to caution us on one point. When you are praying or interceding it is very important not to be judgmental. Remember, mercy triumphs over judgment. Our desire should always be to walk in humility with the love of the Father orchestrating our moves, intercession and prayers. For God so loved the world that He gave His only beloved son. Our heart should be motivated by His heart.

Bonnie Inkster

$\mathcal{9}$. Identify

Now let's look at the book of Daniel chapter nine once more and a little more in depth. In this chapter Daniel had been reading the book of Jeremiah and it is revealed to him that the seventy years of captivity for Jerusalem was over. The thing is: the captivity was over but that did not equate to the Israelites automatically receiving entrance to the land. So what did Daniel do next?

With all prophecy there needs to be revelation, interpretation and then application. In receiving this revelation Daniel then does something about it. His interpretation is that if the seventy years of captivity is over, then God will be true to his word and return the people to their land. Daniel's next step, his application, is to stand in the gap and intercede. Remember: prayer moves God.

Daniel's type of intercession is specific in that he began to confess his sin and the sin of the nation. Take note of verse twenty of chapter nine: "While I was speaking and praying, confessing my sin and the sin of my people Israel and making my request to the Lord my God for his holy hill — while I was still in prayer, Gabriel, the man I had seen in the earlier vision, came to me in swift flight about the time of the evening sacrifice. He instructed me and said to me, "Daniel, I have now come to give you insight and understanding. As soon as you began to pray, a word went out, which I have come to tell you, for you are highly esteemed."

> *With all prophecy there needs to be the revelation, then interpretation followed by application.*

Daniel was praying, interceding and repenting for his sin and the sin of the nation. Daniel would have been in his early teens when Israel went into captivity. However, he did not theologically challenge the issue of repenting and asking God to forgive him and the nation for sins of rebellion, for not listening, for being unfaithful, for being disobedient, for not turning from sin and giving attention to truth. No, Daniel goes on and on identifying with the sin of his ancestors and the people that were in the land. This type of intercession is called identificational repentance or identificational confession.

> *Effectual prayers identify with the ones being prayed for.*

Do you see that Daniel did not separate himself from the sin of the nation but identified with it? The word, identify, means to closely associate with, to regard oneself as sharing in the same characteristics or thinking as someone else. We all have sinned and fallen short of the glory of God. Therefore, like Jesus who identified himself with humanity, we too identify with the sin committed in and on the land.

When the Lord reveals sin, it requires repentance. However, we don't sit in judgment but we confess it as our own and stand in the gap and take it on as our own. We have repented of terrible atrocities across nations. Have we been responsible for them? No! But since we are human, we have the same capability to sin. Therefore, we repent and ask the

Lord to forgive us because mercy triumphs over judgment.

Notice that in Daniel's prayer he often reminds the Lord that he is merciful and forgiving. God longs to forgive and release his loving kindness and tender mercies to us. But remember we have an enemy who uses sin as an access point to steal, kill and destroy. When sin is repented of and the blood of Jesus applied to that sin, God forgives, cleanses and restores. Mercy reigns!

The blood of Jesus has paid for all our sins, iniquities and transgressions. Once the repentance is complete we need to take hold of the blood that Jesus poured out for us. To "plead the blood" is a phrase we used to hear a lot but not so much now a days. This is court language. A judge may ask how do you plead? Well, in the case of sin we plead His blood.   In other words, we are innocent and the enemy can no long use this against us. The thing is Satan is a legalist but the blood is enough! Use the blood of Jesus as 1 John 1: 7&9. Together they say this: "If we confess our sins, He is faithful and just and will forgive us our sin and purify us from all unrighteousness and the blood of Jesus purifies us from all sin". Jesus blood paid for it all, so once we confess our sin we take hold of the blood of Jesus to purify what requires purifying.

Let me give you an example. In Malachi 4:6 it says: "He will turn the hearts of the fathers to the children and the hearts of the children to the fathers; or I will come and strike the land with a curse".

In reading this you might be quickened by just looking at the devastation of the family unit in our western society. So you begin to pray and stand in the gap for families. In doing so, you

Righteousness cloaked in mercy brings hope to those who are hopeless.

begin to ask God to forgive you for ...abandonment, selfishness, abuse, destructive words, pain of divorce, rejection... this list would go on until there was nothing else that was being revealed to you at this time. If praying with a group, then be sure everyone feels it is completed. Then remind the Lord of His word, that He is faithful and just to forgive us of all of our sins and then declare that the blood of Jesus cleans and purifies us from all unrighteousness. Now ask God to turn the hearts of the father to the children and the children to the fathers, to restore families and heal the broken hearted.

This is true identification if you repent for what has happened in families rather than judge them. Through this God can move, releasing his mercy and grace. We can then expect to see traceable changes start to happen in the reporting on families within our society. Righteousness cloaked in mercy brings hope to those who are hopeless. That is our goal with this type of prayer.

Bonnie Inkster

*10.*Prayer and Prophetic Acts

As prophetic people God often calls us to act out things in the natural that clarify what is happening in the spirit. 1 Corinthians 15:46 says, "the spiritual did not come first but the natural and after that the spiritual". As a people of faith we are asked to call things that are not as though they were. These two acts, the doing and the speaking often work together.

In Acts 21:11 we see Agabus taking Paul's belt and tying up his hands and feet before he prophesied over him that the Jewish leaders in Jerusalem

Doing and speaking work together.

would bind him and hand him over to the Gentiles. This was a prophetic act. When we pray we are often lead to act out what is happening.

When I was in England and first started to pray in the nations I was told through a prophetic person to take stakes, put them in the ground and stake out territory for the Lord. We would write scriptures on stakes and drive them into the soil. On our first trip, one lovely fellow got stakes for our team that were two feet long and an inch square. We wrote scriptures on all four sides and took a sledgehammer to stake them into the ground. With our first stake we were on the beach in France for a long time. It was hilarious watching us trying to get that stake in the ground.

You may ask why did we do that? It was an act of faith and obedience. We believe that when we do what is asked of us it makes a difference and something is transpiring here on earth as it is in heaven. Now in regard to the stakes we have gotten smarter. We now use stir sticks. Much easier to transport, carry and put in the ground!

In Joshua 4, Joshua is told to appoint twelve men to carry a stone out of the middle of the river. Why? These stones were to serve as a remembrance and as a sign amount the young of the nation. In various places we have been told to gather stones and build a memorial. Do we think these stones have power? No! But we know that God does and He will use whatever He tells us to do.

We also use salt. Salt began as an act of obedience with me. I felt the Lord say salt the ground as you pray, throw salt into water, on the ground, in buildings... take it with you when you pray on the land and in the nations. Salt is used for seasoning, preserving and

> *Prayer is an act of faith and obedience.*

disinfecting. The New Testament refers to us as being the salt of the earth and we are told to have our conversation seasoned with salt. Why? Because we are called to season, preserve and disinfect! The Old Testament has an interesting use of salt. In 2 Kings 2:19-22 we see that Elisha was asked to help because the city had a problem. Their particular issue was with the water; it was "bad and the land unproductive". This city was Jericho. Joshua had cursed it when Israel entered the promise land and began to possess it. We see in Joshua 6:26..."cursed be the man before the Lord who rises up and builds this city Jericho; he shall lay it's foundation with his firstborn and with his youngest he shall set up its gates". This curse had its effect in the days of Hiel of Bethel as you can see in 1Kings 16:34. Hiel did rebuild the city at the expense of losing two sons! However, it didn't mean that the curse was gone and this is why the men of Jericho came to Elisha. Now, let's look at what he did. Elisha called for a new bowl and salt. I want to discuss salt.

Salt spoke of covenant with God and of judgment. In Judges 9:45 we see that Abimelech defeated and demolished a city and then sowed it with salt. This speaks of the judgment against the people and land. In Leviticus 2:13 we see that the covenant that God had with his people was always confirmed with salt. When Elisha called for salt he was judging what was afflicting the people and reminding God of His covenant with his people. He was decreeing that the curse that brought death and unproductivity was removed. Elisha threw the salt into the water and declared that it was healed and that never again would it cause death or be unproductive. Elisha used his authority and we too have been given authority. We need to use it. As we go out onto the land we always take salt. It prophetically speaks of breaking the judgment that the blood of Jesus has already secured for us. However, we need to execute that which has been done for us. When we take prayer teams to pray for the land, we take salt with the knowledge that as we sprinkle it God will heal the land and cause His blessing to flow.

As you are led to do something, you may wonder what good does it do. However, when you respond to the spirit and act, you will release something that will bring a shift here on earth. I want to encourage you to be a person of faith and act on what you are hearing and like Elisha prophecy the solution.

11. Conclusion

Ephesians 6:18 says, 'pray in the Spirit on all occasions with all kinds of prayers and requests. With this in mind, be alert and always keep on praying for all the Lord's people'. Paul encourages us with a few final directives. First off, we are directed to pray in the Spirit. He actually says to pray this way on all occasions. He says in 1 Corinthians 14:15 to pray in the spirit and pray with your understanding. In other words do both.

Our understanding is limited. Our thoughts are not His thoughts it says in Isaiah 55:8 but we are told in Romans 8:26-27 that the Spirit himself intercedes for us. The Spirit intercedes through us in accordance to the will of God. Therefore, we pray in the Spirit knowing that God is at work and he will work everything together for good and bring the good work He has begun to completion.

The second instruction given to us by Paul is to pray with our understanding. Even though we don't know the whole picture or how God is going to work we pray with the understanding we have. Having done so, we trust in God to do what only He can do. That takes faith!

Faith is the currency of heaven. Without faith it's impossible to please God but with faith you can move mountains! Nothing is impossible with God! We must believe that or prayer is just a religious action and a waste of time. But since you walk in faith and have faith, know that God is at work to bring His kingdom here on earth as it is in heaven! He desires to work with YOU to bring about His work here. Partner with Him and you will move mountains and bring down Goliaths!

Be encouraged, be filled with the Spirit

and have faith in God. He is at work to bring His kingdom and He wants to use you to change the world!

ABOUT BONNIE

Bonnie Inkster is an excellent international speaker, teacher and author. She and Jim started a ministry registered with CRA called Worldchangers Canada Society.

In Europe Bonnie taught and mentored in leadership development as an integral member of the core team of leadership colleges established in England. Bonnie initiated a prayer ministry within Europe aimed at resolving past conflict and facilitating peace within 30 countries of the European Union. This involved recruiting volunteers, training them and directing practical applications for their learning.

Her driving motivation is to see people discover their life call, to be equipped for this and experience the potential of their unique gifting. Bonnie has the ability to see what you can be and will inspire and motivate you so you will be encouraged to maximize your impact in whatever field you are working in.